Seas to Mulberries

Poetry by Frank Watson

Edited by Tiara Winter-Schorr

Plum White Press

Published by Plum White Press LLC

For information concerning reprints, email:
followingtheblueflute@gmail.com

ISBN-13: 978-1939832023 (paperback)
ISBN-10: 1939832020 (paperback)
LCCN: 2013921467
BISAC: Poetry / General

Published in the United States of America

Also by Frank Watson

<u>Edited Volumes</u>

Poetry Nook
The dVerse Anthology
One Hundred Leaves
Fragments

Table of Contents

Seas to Mulberries

Micropoetry

I pray in secret
And somehow, somewhere,
I am heard

if you pray
does it matter
if someone hears?

Splendid:
Nighttime walks
And daylight dreams

Shattered,
A rose bleeds raw

This earth in winter,
A frozen hearth

shadowed mystery
walking in silent footsteps

the halo

of our broken souls

In the phantom of sleep
She lures me into
A nymph's erotic dreams

Morning mist
A song from deep
Dark trees

charcoal etched in fog
above the tower lights

an empty path
a river bog
I walk the winter night

How deep was the dye
Of my longing?

A flower appeared,
I went to pluck,
And found just lingering snow.

Translated from the Japanese of an unknown poet in the Kokinshu

A boat becomes the wave
A glow of up and down
In effervescent light

surreptitiously we slip
into the Deep South
amidst the cypress mists

Man is mere delicacy
When kissed by the mosquito
And the mosquito is a lover
When trapped in the spider's net

In my dreams
I build a castle
Where the shadows dance

夢の中
築いた城に
影踊る

The pregnant moon
Sleeps behind
Its saffron veil

A dozen stars outshine
Manhattan's light.

A hundred mountains
And a thousand creeks
Will all fold into one

A bird's squeal
Sails through the morning air
As a river burns

I talk to the dead
With old souls engaged
In a cup of tea

what does she read?

strange woman
with an open book

it's easy to begin
but harder than sin
to stay until the end

to feel vs. to know

does it matter
to the soul?

the other side
where my blue
still waits for you

the curls
of your swirls

I fall, I fall

butterfly madame

spring brings color
to black & white

the clock bell rings

as time unfolds
persistent truth

earth rolls over
as the orange-red sun
begins to sink beneath
the mountain line

you sing
a discordant song
while I play along

if I whisper
will you come back
in silence?

I don't know
whether you're
water or wine

it is true?
you were always
as you were

the rust
in your voice
consumes the trust

brooks murmur,
wheat whistles
a tune from God

the release
of your hooks
and what is left?

I see you
in white silhouette

is there still time?

slipping into your hills
when all of time
is bent

brush me with
your loose-
leaf kiss

three houses
and we are
still apart

after you were gone
only the mask
was left

the blackest black
of your desires
will bring me back

stranger in the room

I hear
a chance remark

memory and fate

I did not know
what I had lost

Is there something
you wanted to say?

Your eyes speak
but your lips escape

in silence

the girl became
her mother's
violin lessons

now I am a tree
but once
I roamed free

in your mind
I find sunflower seeds
to my thoughts

the window
became abstract art
but not for the bird

he is damned

but thought he saw
the symbol

to his delusion

in rags
I picked out
virtue's scent

the moonlight's
twilight vines

forever tether me
to earth

why did Eve
conceal a smile
when she plucked
the fruit?

they danced
under a tree,
tomorrow unseen

her skin sang
librettos
with every move

she dreamed of snow,
he dreamed of beach

a peaceful glow
they could not reach

in the rumor mill
I hear the singing
of a little bird

all of tomorrow
wrapped in a
lacquered box

moss-brushed stones,
painted river tones
a rowboat all alone

the horse munches grass
without a thought
to what will pass

patient, aged woman

—Exhibit A—

her only wish
was for the doctors
to learn her name

step by step
down the lower
rungs of life

she strung together
seashells and found
what she had lost

I never knew
what a fine man he was
until he died

while he lived
we could not tell
the good
from the evil

time slips through
the sweetest grips

illusion of desire

I walk the scales
until I ascend
into her tune

woman of earth
and mountain,
clay and fire

I shall remain
through all the seasons

the white dandelion's
electric hair
brings light to
black night air

woman of raisins
and molasses

cinnamon-toasted
lips I taste
with every lick

a crime
is no less a crime

when done
a thousand times

she and I
are not the same
but yet . . .

a cup of tea

laughing
at the rumors

she knows
to be true

as if by smoke,
we became friends

through the
endless nights

on crutches
she somehow
reaches the clouds

she covers herself
but the lips
still ask for more

Where is this place
That waits in far off grace?

Oh, fertile earth
I welcome your rebirth

the lady of the sky
leans down to kiss me
with her big blue eyes

she was
too much blue
for his
plain brown

the clouds preached
in a booming voice

and all at once

the crow congregation
rose to the altar

he sucked on ice
until it seeped
into his veins
and froze
his heart

Flowers slipped
and melted into earth

touched within
they grew again

I fall into
the dustbin of sleep

and swirl about

to awake

renewed

the heart renews
from the place
you least expect

how quickly
the honor
of the dead
dissolve
into life's river

false philosophy

master of a truth
that no one knows

the philosopher
spun a tune

but his only audience
was the midnight moon

life and dust
bewitched together
in the smoke of time

they lay flowers
but still
she looks at me

how the cold air
slipped the sun's
embrace

to go on a journey
a thousand miles away

the wind stopped

as the hanging sheets
carried memories
of the night before

I waited in the dark
until the raven's

beating beating

sound
sent shivers
to my bones

tiny embers
that flew
through still air

to ignite a wildfire
across the dead land

holding
the instrument
prepared for battle

my angry muse

blue head
gold limbs
emerald sides

god
of a million years

weighing the words

the entombed
will rise in triumph

I am a flute player
playing my tune
with nowhere else to go

impatient
she wants more
than a simple glance

her pen
wrote symbols
seared into my skin
like a broken tattoo

dark and chilling
night engulfs

she lays
a single feather
across my skull

senseless
to the sting

broken
to the bone

dark side
of the moon

jewel from
another tune

I knew her once
but now she is just
smoke & wind

Flowers point
To garden snow

Vanished in the storm
Passing away

Perhaps
It was me?

Translated from the Japanese of Fujiwara no Kintsune (1171-1244)

he pulled
a dead man's hand
with fate sealed
in desert sand

we share our skin

I see the world
through you

a whole continent

told
through

a cup of tea

on the edge
of earth

the water
sinks

into the abyss

polar images
as darkness
turns to light

wave energy
contains the pulse
of what we say

but not
our humanity

the water is warm

I drift
in the pleasant dream
of its embrace

I touch the mirror
but what I sought
is not there

I paint and paint
but her room is never
what it used to be

the road
connects two cliffs

supported by
a spirit
I do not know

a string
of butterflies
shapes the air
with every flutter
of a kiss

fertile water
sprinkles my mind:

a new life

beauty dies
in twilight shrouds

but midnight stars
emblaze the night

till dawn
once more ignites

in the thicket
of her voice

the nails dug
deep into
my parched skin

life
is a duality
of dream

of blood and feast,
of ecstasy and pain

till in the field
we're lain

the violinist
has the face
of a

black-and-white
mime

Full-bodied woman,
drunk of the moon

devil, prisoner
to your kiss:

I'm doomed

we bond
a million times
with each departure

three ladies dance:

a devil
an angel
and the one I love

alone in the woods
she waits

he's almost there

entranced
by the way her fingers
move the instrument

one heart
in the blue sea

a moonlit reflection

water freezes
the land

my still heart

I walk into
your eyes
and sail into
the light
blue sky

into the night
the streetlight
haunts
what little remains

angel tears
but in her eyes
a demon look

her tears
stand still
with a question

the lion crouches

two lovers
reflect in his eyes

ravished
in the woods

the smell of daisies

the bee's
bitter kiss

in the orchid's
embrace

a mirror reflection

where did he go?

the flowers
no longer bloom

they carry me
ashore
but I keep looking back

she opened
her treasure box

but found
what she'd prefer
to forget

it was her destiny
to forget

but he
would always
remember

she blew in
on a seashell

but the storm
would lead me
astray

people behind
glass mirrors
and stories untold

his final wish
was for a blanket
to stay warm

the sunrise
sprinkles golden dust
in morning love

nighttime rainbow
in a lightning storm

drawn to your sign

her mouth
contained all
the secrets

but the mystery
was always mine

a boat
under the moon
is seeking the way home

dark waves
eternal sea

she welcomes me
to a dance

a picnic
in Eden's spring

she stands
hair strewn
on seaside rocks

and prays
to the goddess
of wind

blinded
by the vision
drawing close

and the presence
of God

the church steeple
spirals up
like the trees below

spring love

all drunk
on the same water

the crafty banker
lives in a
very
very
small house

disordered
magic
when our lips brush

but how
did it get this far?

nude
she looks
out the window

her lover's gone
with the early dawn

it's afternoon
and still she waits
forlorn

abandoned
house where only
the children go to play

in piracies &
haunted days

green path
sky blue
girl in orange
pink kiss
red red red

in the courtyard
Venus and her maids
were nude

but is it lewd
to allude to gods
whose breasts protrude?

through a gateway
I saw Constantinople

ancient church
through an
ancient mosque

tulips grow
new life

forgotten grave

the grandfather
looks at the boy in shorts
he once knew

the villa floor
was half-completed
before Vesuvius

drunken elves
that roam at night

the midnight garden
has come to life

the crow squawked
but the scarecrow
stood his ground

some take
criticism well

leaning back
she covers
her pale breasts

but when will he
make his move?

blue seas
crumble cliffs

white sand
watchtower
stands alone

the organ
vibrates
long after
the church door
has shut

chained soul
never lets go

comrade
on the road
to time's decay

sleep overruns

half-awake
I wonder
what I done

immortal wings
carry clouds astray

dark rain
on a summer's day

white bones
on the living room floor

no attic
can contain
the secrets we hold

uneven breath

you step
I'm drunk

your scent's
enough

a windowsill
bottle collects
the light

lingering bloom,
a starless night

a hundred years' war

enemies exist
and they're inside

she will fling
my ashes to the sea
as a cool wind blows

and I shall return
to nature

a spirit
a child free

crying slaves
iron-beaten
bones

blood-soaked
chains

we strain
we strain
to break their reign

I placed my trust
in gold and wine

and never found
a thing divine

our blood
may all be red

but we'll still be filed
& categorized

until we're dead

what is heaven
without a taste
of hell?

she fell
before the last
musical chair
had disappeared

the bare-back
sofa was not meant
for human rest

in her rowboat
the lady paddles out

white dress

reflected
moonlight shine

the atoms
of our time dissolve
together in fog

gauze silk
wisp of wind

I see a hint
of shadow
skin

when you loitered

I pushed you
and my life
astray

what does she see
in this dark night
as she looks
out to sea?

still playing the violin
after all these years
of no one listenin'

on a night
when everyone
is dancing

a lone woman
prays

looking away
from the wind

her eyes
blow through me

desert wind
sand dunes
from another time

earth swims
in a rolling quake
around the fire rim

heaven is far
and hell is dim

living soul

the sun rises
from a dying night

Knowing Yesterday
Knowing Tomorrow

The Burning, Burning Sun

she prays
to a wall
that will not answer
back

as the wind blows
a lone tree
bends into the night

liquid notes
sail past
the midnight moon

the masks
fail to convey
the tragedy inside

one eye
half-awake
the other screams

he played
until he was
the song

and knew
neither happiness
nor desire

withered memories
and new ones born

there's nothing in life
I wish to scorn

slayed by
the blades of eros

I open my chest
to be flayed
a thousand times more

I said goodbye
to the cactus sand

but could not forget
my wounded hands

falling on
my granite heart
the virgin snow

he dreamed in roses
without knowing
what it meant

on the rock
summit of my life
volcanic fire

vultures search
for a golden heart

the things we've lost

sea wind blows
in whimsical flight

my mast in throes
of her delight

In this desert
of sand and wind

I am neither man
nor spirit
between the worlds

bound
to the searing
rock embrace

desert woman
of the sand

your shadow
touches
an outstretched hand

desert ghost
your howls
scatter in the wind

in the wind
a lost girl

floating blonde
will o' wisp

mouth sealed
eyes closed
hair flows

you speak
a shadow wind

remembering all
when nothing
remembered is true

on the balcony
she looks through the door
of another balcony

twilight
in New York

バルコニー隣家のドアを君眺む薄明かりなるニューヨークにて

Translated into Japanese by @tomcat_com, used with permission

led astray
by the waning moon

sly devil
with her sweet,
misleading tune

she worships
the blood tears
in his eyes

she sacrificed
a life of roses

but was left
strung up
with nowhere to go

hiding behind
a curtain
when night
falls dark
and low

it was a parlor trick
but the ball rolled
and never came back

latching onto clouds
when nothing stops
my fall to ground

she points

as everything
floats away

and I wear
a stupid grin

there was only
one shoe left

and no one
in the distance

in silhouette
the curtain hides only
the details

all quiet
in the valley
of shadows

so why do I
enter with caution?

the joker
wanted
to say more

but the cat
had cut his tongue

the corroded foundation
has left the house
facing
the oddest direction

a paper sheet
is all that stops
the cold, wet wind

the empty man
sat in his chair

with few objects
in his room

the wall
I climb
is too bare
for burgled
dreams

fire burns
until the oxygen
is gone

where from the ashes
will life be drawn?

the old man
creates a marionette
of the young man
he once was

falling and falling
toward dawn
I kiss her goodbye
and welcome
the sun

he is with me as I walk
he is with me as I talk

in the valley of shadows
I go wherever the wind
shall blow

War
for so many tribes
and yet there is only one

humanity prescribes
what cannot be done

her shadow scars
still hide the memories
of love undone

I am so small
as the dust storm
broods over me

the clay city
draws me toward
its parched horizon

on a forest walk
I hear the bell ring
and stop
to see
the wind-touched leaves

I touch the silk
and remember
what happened
a long time ago

secrets of the dark
are best remembered
in the dark

the bottle opened
and the world slipped out

my feet unwashed

cabin in the woods

the man had more to fear
than civilization

some stand
and others fall
but none can look away

no one else to play

I ask the clouds
to join in

the elderly couple
still play music

with their broken
instruments

the tormentor sneers

a window
is the only way out

a dark flag
in the light breeze
as twilight nears

silent leaves

a bird trills
in the blanket sun

in the field
a whitewashed skull
a blackened heart

sailing toward
the end of the world

sea monsters
& riddles
& what little we know

arrow across
the midnight moon
I wonder where it'll land

ice within
she drifts away

my melted heart

naked before
the empty plain
he wears the earth

he folds the piano
like a sheet
of desire lost

I saw her
in segments
that made her smile

she's trying to draw me
into her ruined
little town

in history
there is little
but ruined towns

and clouds
that tell a story

numb

the boat
will never come

to this forgotten
shore

echoes
of the way we pray

journey
to another life

a skeletal man
escapes
from the village
of lost souls

the rose bones
seal his fate

in the petals
of entrapment

she compartmentalized
until no one was sure
who she was

Is it spring?

The plums bloom late
And not even
The warblers
Will sing their tune.

Translated from the Japanese of Fujiwara no Kotonao

Spring begins though
Snow is falling still

The cuckoo
Sings a cry
On a plum tree bough

Translated from the Japanese of an unknown poet in the Kokinshu

Spring begins
In the midst of snow

Perhaps now, at last,
The bush warbler's
Frozen tears will melt.

Translated from the Japanese of Fujiwara no Takaiko (842-910)

On snow falling

Spring mist sweeps
Through budding leaves

But in the village
Where the snow fell
The fallen flowers weep.

Translated from the Japanese of Ki no Tsurayuki (872-945)

Gazing at the Moon, Longing from Afar

The sea gives birth
To a shining moon
As the other end of the world
Shares this moment.

This sentimental man
Resents the distant night
And the whole evening
Gives rise to longing.

Extinguishing a candle,
Feeling the fullness of moonlight;
Putting on clothes
As I wake in heavy dew.

Unable to fill my hands
With this gift
I return to bed
And dream a lovely tryst.

Translated from the Chinese of Zhang Jiuling (678-740)

Delighted to See My Cousin, Only to Say "Goodbye" Again

Ten years
Of chaos left behind;
Growing throughout,
We come across one another.

Inquiring on our family names,
Surprised, we begin to see;
We state our names
And reflect upon our changed appearances.

Coming and going, forever changing:
Seas to mulberries, mulberries to seas.
Our words cease
By the evening bell.

Tomorrow,
The path to Baling,
The autumn mountains,
And once again we part.

Translated from the Chinese of Li Yi (746-829).

"Seas to mulberries, mulberries to seas" is an idiom reflecting how greatly things can change over time.

Enjoying a Visit with My Cousin Lu Lun

Quiet night, all around
There are no neighbors,
Living in isolation
On the family's ancient farm.

In the midst of rain,
A tree with yellow leaves;
Beneath a lantern,
This white-haired man.

Because I am alone,
Sinking with the time,
I often feel ashamed
When you see me.

All our lives
We have shared a friendship,
Bonded, moreover,
Like the cousins Cai.

Translated from the Chinese of Sikong Shu (720-790)

Sikong makes an allusion to the Cai cousins, historical figures known for the tightness of their bond.

Northern Wind

Hand in hand I travel,
Torrential rain and snow:

The northern wind is cold
And so my joy does grow.
Is it all in vain? Am I wrong?
No—for I am left alone.

Hand in hand returning,
Falling rain and snow:

The northern wind has melody,
And so my joy does grow.
Is it all in vain? Am I wrong?
No—for I am left alone.

There are no bandits, red as a fox,
There are no bandits, black as a crow:

And so my joy does grow
As I walk together with my cart.
Is it all in vain? Am I wrong?
No—for I am left alone.

Translated from an anonymous Chinese poem in the Shijing

Ballad of the Three States

Wartime efforts are pure
For the three hundred that depart to heaven,
Grasping a lonely cloud by the sides,
Becoming one with the sky.

For the golden child, the mountains
And water make a treacherous path;
And as a snake studies the bird in his cage,
So power flows from heaven.

Translated from an anonymous Chinese poem in the Shijing

Temple of the Shu-Han Dynasty's First Lord

Among heaven and earth, a heroic spirit
Inspired awe for a thousand years.

When power divided, like a three-legged cauldron,
He restored the Han Dynasty's coinage.

The Prime Minister created a state
But the emperor's son was unworthy.

Miserable, dreary Shu:
Your dancers danced
Before the Palace of Wei.

Translated from the Chinese of Liu Yuxi (772-842)

This is a historical poem, telling the story of the rise and fall of the Shu-Han Kingdom (221-263 AD). This kingdom was founded by Liu Bei (the "First Lord" in the title) after the fall of the Han Dynasty (206 BC – 220 AD). As Liu Bei was directly related to the royal family of the Han Dynasty, it can be seen as an attempt to restore the failed dynasty, alluded to in the line, "He restored the Han Dynasty's coinage."

The Shu-Han Kingdom was one of the kingdoms competing for control over all of China during the Three Kingdoms period (220-280). The other two were the Wei and the Wu kingdoms. The poet, Liu Yuxi, alludes to this as power divided into a three-legged cauldron, a suggestive image with the internal boiling representing the struggles of the time.

While Liu Bei and his Prime Minister, Zhuge Liang, successfully created the state, the emperor's son was incompetent. He was suspected of being mentally handicapped, but in any case lived for pleasure without paying attention to the affairs of state.

Finally, in 263 AD, the Wei Kingdom conquered the Shu-Han Kingdom, referred to in the line about the Shu-Han's dancers dancing before the Wei Palace.

Song of an Old Cypress

Before the Kongming Temple
Lies an ancient cypress
With boughs of bronze
And roots of rock.

Its frosty skin rains down,
Encircling the span of forty arms;
Its dark green leaves can reach
Some two thousand feet of sky.

Ministers and rulers
Had set a time to meet
And the trees they left behind,
The locals revered.

Clouds are coming now, bringing an air
That sits about the Witch's Gorge
While the moon sends a cold that passes
The mountain's snowy white.

~~

I recall in former times the path
Around the Brocade Pavilion, to the east.

Lord Liu Bei and Kongming,
Both enshrined, now reside in that hall.

On a lofty mountain, the trunks and
Branches reach the ancient plains;
And there are paintings, sweet and graceful,
Shown through the windows of an empty shrine.

~~

Sinking, dropping, seizing land,
As though he holds the earth;
Tall, alone, among a sky
That's vast and deep, with many winds.

A power sustaining him,
Brilliant and divine,
Standing upright,
A primal source,
A feat of Nature.

A great building will tilt
Without its pillars and poles
But ten thousand pulling bulls
Could turn their necks in vain,
For he is a heavy mountain.

He did not show his culture to the world,
Yet has already startled it;
And he cannot avoid being cut down,
But who will do it?

How can his bitter core escape
The crickets and ants?
A phoenix passes through
The sweet smelling leaves to rest.

Men of purpose and those withdrawn
Do not complain, alas!
Since ancient times, those of great talent
Have found it hard to be of use.

Translated from the Chinese of Du Fu (712-770)

This poem talks about a cypress tree, symbolizing virtuous men like Kongming, the honorific name of Zhuge Liang, an outstanding statesman from Chinese history. Du Fu wrote this poem in 766, when the An Lushan Rebellion (755-763) had been put down, but China was still under attack by various barbarian groups. He was lamenting that China had talented men willing to serve the country, but did not take advantage of their services.

Your Eyes Are Blue

Your eyes are blue and, when you laugh,
their smooth clarity reminds me
of the trembling brilliance of morning
    reflected in the sea.

Your eyes are blue and, when you cry,
their transparent tears
contain the dew drops
    upon a violet.

Your eyes are blue and, if in their depths
an idea shines like a point of light,
it seems to me a lost star
    in the evening sky.

*Translated from the Spanish of Gustavo Adolfo Bécquer (1836-1870),
which was, in turn, inspired by Lord Byron's (1788-1824) "I Saw Thee
Weep" from* Hebrew Melodies.

Subway to the Center of the Earth

Groaning men
and tracks

of women who know
the carnal gaze

of tattooed jazz
in deep bass

as we're heading down
a heated core

the violent shore
of tribal pound

a prophet's sound
that says...
       we're
          m
            e
              l
                t
              i n g

down a hole
of earthly flesh

with three stops left

Meditation on Weeds

A micropoetry sequence

In a settled age
We make our clothes
Of the thickest weeds

We live in a landscape
Of yellow, the sky
Embalmed in weeds

We plant the seeds,
But what remains?
The taker's weeds

We must cross
A bridge
That's grown of weeds

For nature knows not
The iris from the weed

And from the fattest soil
Grows the richest
Weeds

An Old-Fashioned Love Story

A micropoetry sequence

a knight
without a boat
could see a tower
on the other side
of the water

> he made it
> to the tower
> but there was neither
> damsel nor
> door to enter

the damsel
had seen the knight
approaching
and moved
to another tower

> no damsel
> in the tower,
> the knight
> went searching
> for another

Credits

"she and I" appeared in *Prune Juice,* Vol. 11, 2013.

"Song of an Old Cypress" appeared in *Rosebud,* Vol. 54.

"Subway to the Center of the Earth" appeared in *Bora,* Vol. 2.

About the Author

Frank Watson was born in Venice, California and now lives in New York City. He enjoys literature, art, calligraphy, history, jazz, international culture, and travel.

His books include *Fragments: poetry, ancient & modern* (editor), *One Hundred Leaves: a new, annotated translation of the* Hyakunin Isshu (editor and translator), and *The dVerse Anthology: Voices of Contemporary World Poetry* (editor). He is also editor of the monthly journal of poetry and art, *Poetry Nook*. His work has appeared in various literary journals, anthologies, e-zines, and literary blogs.

Poetry Blog: www.followtheblueflute.com

Twitter: @FollowBlueFlute

Made in the USA
Lexington, KY
27 November 2013